# Energy

Suzanne Barchers

## Consultants

**Sally Creel, Ed.D.**
Curriculum Consultant

**Leann Iacuone, M.A.T., NBCT, ATC**
Riverside Unified School District

**Image Credits:** p.10 Image Source Plus/Alamy; p.23 Image Source/Alamy; p.27 Angela Hampton Picture Library/Alamy; pp.28–29 (illustrations) J.J. Rudisill; all other images from Shutterstock.

**Library of Congress Cataloging-in-Publication Data**

Barchers, Suzanne I., author.
Energy / Suzanne Barchers ; consultant, Sally Creel, Ed.D., curriculum consultant, Leann Iacuone, M.A.T., NBCT, ATC Riverside Unified School District, Jill Tobin, California Teacher of the Year semi-finalist, Burbank Unified School District.
pages cm
Summary: "Energy is all around you. Energy is there when you run and play. Energy is there when you sleep, too. There are many types of energy."
— Provided by publisher.
Audience: K to grade 3.
Includes index.
ISBN 978-1-4807-4605-3 (pbk.)
ISBN 978-1-4807-5072-2 (ebook)
1. Force and energy—Juvenile literature. I. Title.
QC73.4.B367 2015
531.6—dc23
2014014171

**Teacher Created Materials**
5301 Oceanus Drive
Huntington Beach, CA 92649-1030
http://www.tcmpub.com

**ISBN 978-1-4807-4605-3**

# Table of Contents


Energy All Around You . . . . . . . . . . . . . . . 4

How Does Energy Work? . . . . . . . . . . . . . . 6

Keep Moving! . . . . . . . . . . . . . . . . . . . . . 12

That Is Hot! . . . . . . . . . . . . . . . . . . . . . . 18

Electricity and Magnetism . . . . . . . . . . . 22

Working for You . . . . . . . . . . . . . . . . . . . 26

Let's Do Science! . . . . . . . . . . . . . . . . . . 28

Glossary. . . . . . . . . . . . . . . . . . . . . . . . . 30

Index . . . . . . . . . . . . . . . . . . . . . . . . . . 31

Your Turn! . . . . . . . . . . . . . . . . . . . . . . . 32

# Energy All Around You

Look around you. Is a computer on? Is a TV on? Listen. Can you hear kids talking? Can you hear lights humming?

The machines and the people are using **energy**. Are you sitting in a chair? Are you quiet? You are still using energy.

# How Does Energy Work?

You know what it means to **work**. You work at school and at playing sports. You may work at playing the piano. You may work on chores at home.

In science, work means making something happen. Each time you take a breath, your body is at work. Even when you sleep, your body is at work. All of this work takes energy.

## Listen Up!

When you talk, you move the air. Those waves of **sound energy** reach your eardrums. That is how you hear.

# Hello, Sunshine!

Energy comes from many sources. One source is always working for us—the sun. The sun is full of energy. Without the sun, we could not live on Earth.

The sun sends us both heat and light. Plants use the sun's **light energy** to grow. When you eat plants, that energy is passed to you.

People and animals get energy from the food they eat. Plants get energy from the sun.

# Rise and Shine!

Do you ever wake up and still feel tired? Your body needs energy, just like a car needs gas. The sun's energy is stored in the food you eat.

Once you eat, your body gets to work. You use more energy when you are active. If you are not active, the food's energy is stored inside your body.

Energy is stored within fat cells in your body.

## Inside Scoop

**Chemical energy** is found in food and gas. Do you have a flashlight? The chemicals in the batteries have energy.

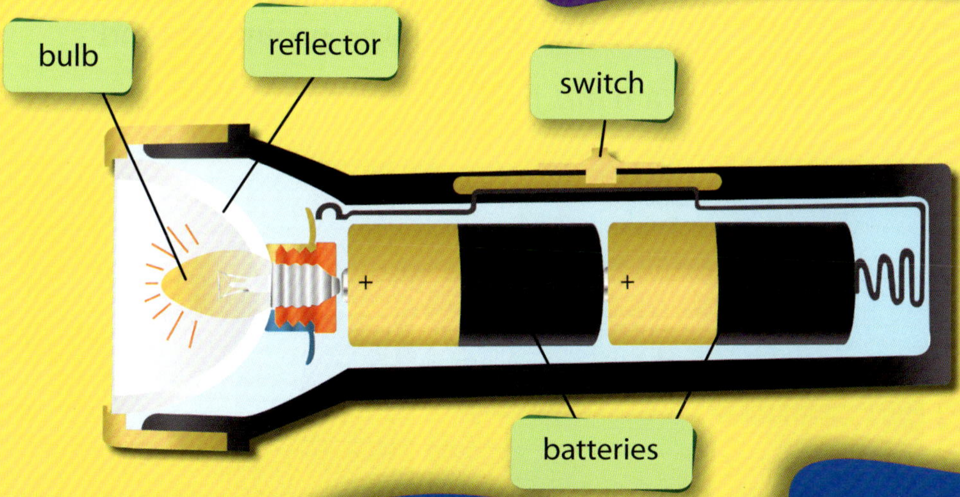

# Keep Moving!

A lot of energy comes through motion. So, wind up and read on!

## Wind Power

Look outside. Is the wind blowing? People have used wind power for thousands of years. Wind can move a sailing ship, and windmills once were used to pump water and grind corn.

You might see wind turbines near your home. They use wind to make electricity. A large group of wind turbines is called a *wind farm*.

Turbines turn the wind's energy into electricity.

# Water Power

Water has power, just like the wind does. Years ago, waterwheels were used. They work much like windmills. The flow of the water turns machines.

A dam on a lake also makes power. It holds back the water. The water is released through pipes. The water has energy when it flows. It can be used to make electricity.

## Store It for Later

The water held in a dam has stored energy. The energy is waiting to be used.

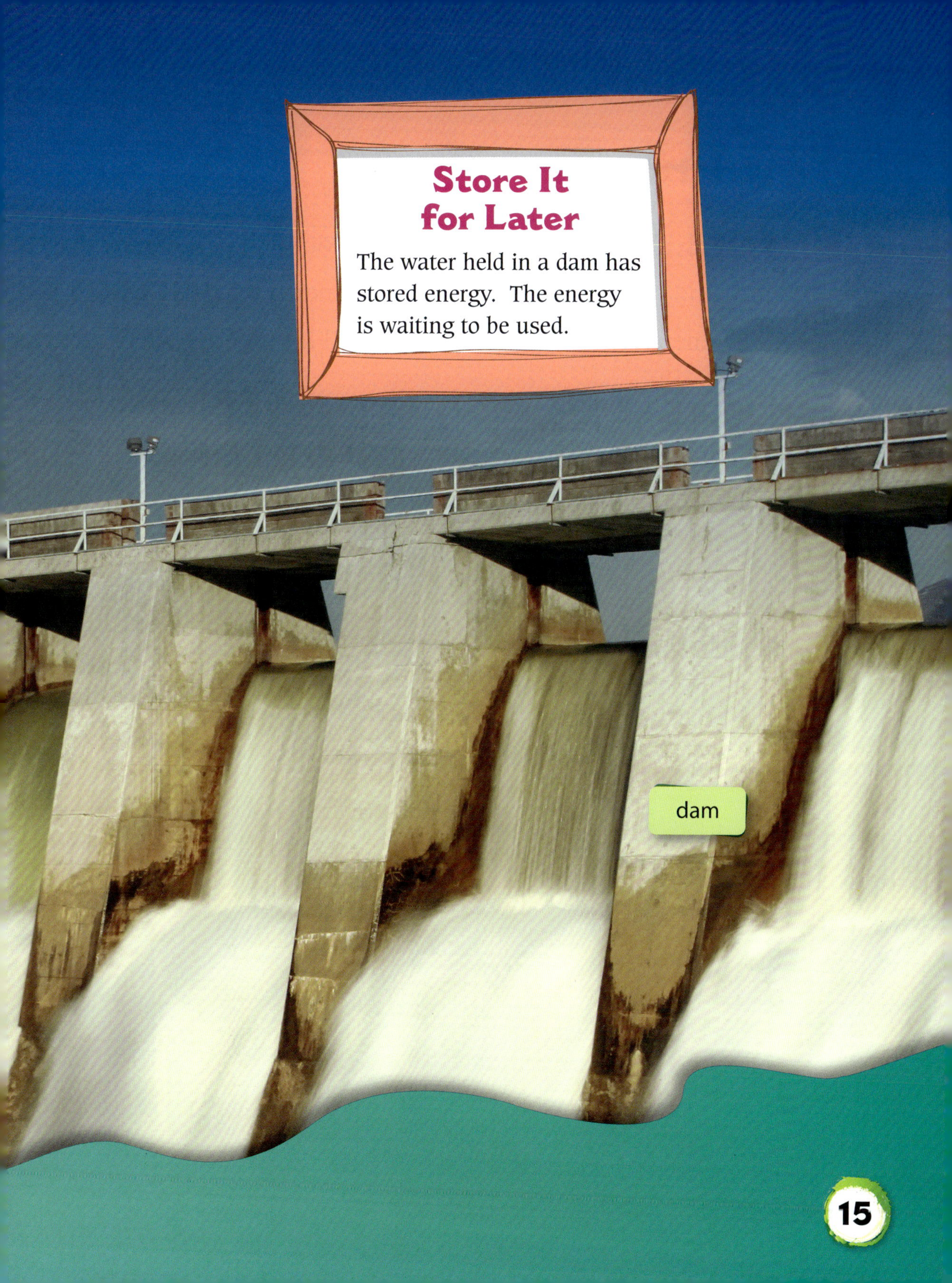

# Moving On

Think about what happens when you hit a ball. Hit it hard, and it flies. But there is more energy at work than just the energy from your arm. The ball has energy while it moves.

Things that move have moving energy. Fast things have more moving energy, and slow things have less.

Which has more moving energy: a plane or a hot-air balloon?

The fastest jet in the world can fly nearly 7,000 miles per hour.

# That Is Hot!

No one knows for sure when fire was first used. We think that it was used by people who lived in caves. Fire gives off heat energy as it burns.

A fire can be used for more than cooking food and keeping warm. A hot fire can be used to make pottery, bend metal, or shape glass.

### Glassmaking

When glass is heated, it can be bent and shaped. It will keep that shape after it cools.

Cave people had very little comfort. Fire was very important for their survival.

# Make Some Heat

You do not need a fire to make heat. Rub your hands together while you count to 20. Your closed hands will feel warm for a few seconds.

When you rub your hands together, you are passing energy. Rubbing two things together causes **friction**. Friction always makes heat. Friction can be used to start a fire.

These people rub two sticks together to make fire.

This boy feels the heat caused by friction when he rubs his hands together.

# Electricity and Magnetism

Here is a neat trick. Rub a balloon on your hair. Then, press the balloon to a wall. It will stick to the wall because of **static electricity**. A lightning bolt is caused by the same kind of electricity.

Walk on a rug with your socks on. You might get a shock. This is caused by static electricity, too.

Static electricity makes this girl's hair stand up.

Find a pair of magnets. Hold them close. They either attract each other or push away. This force is called **magnetism**. You cannot see it, but you can feel it.

Scientists have learned how to use magnetism and electricity. These kinds of energy help keep our lights on and our homes warm.

This girl picks up metal paper clips with a magnet.

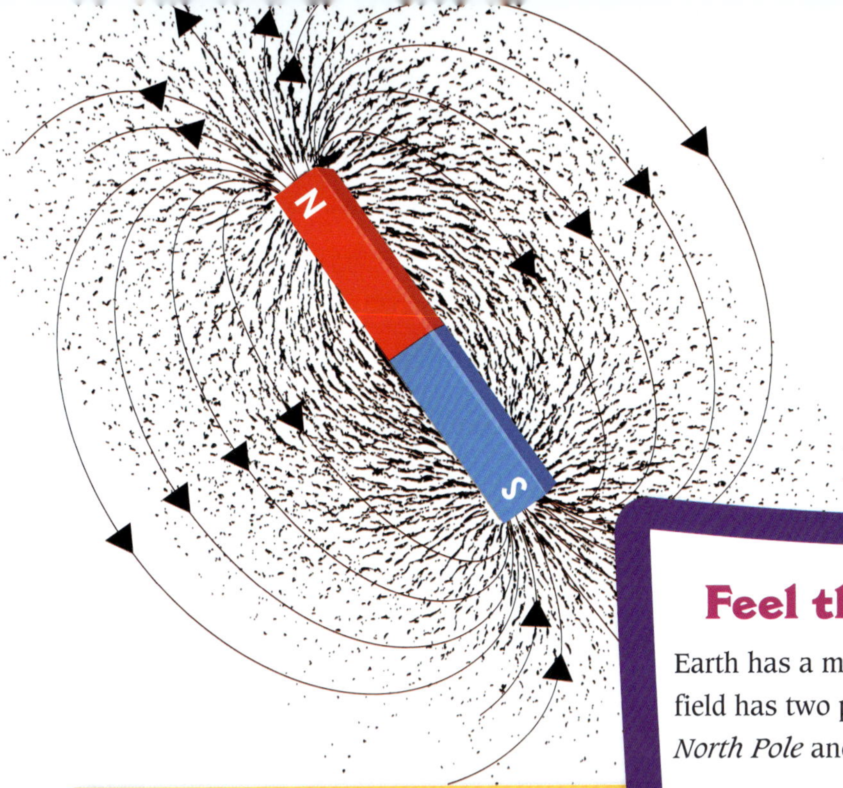


## Feel the Force

Earth has a magnetic field. The field has two poles called the *North Pole* and the *South Pole*.

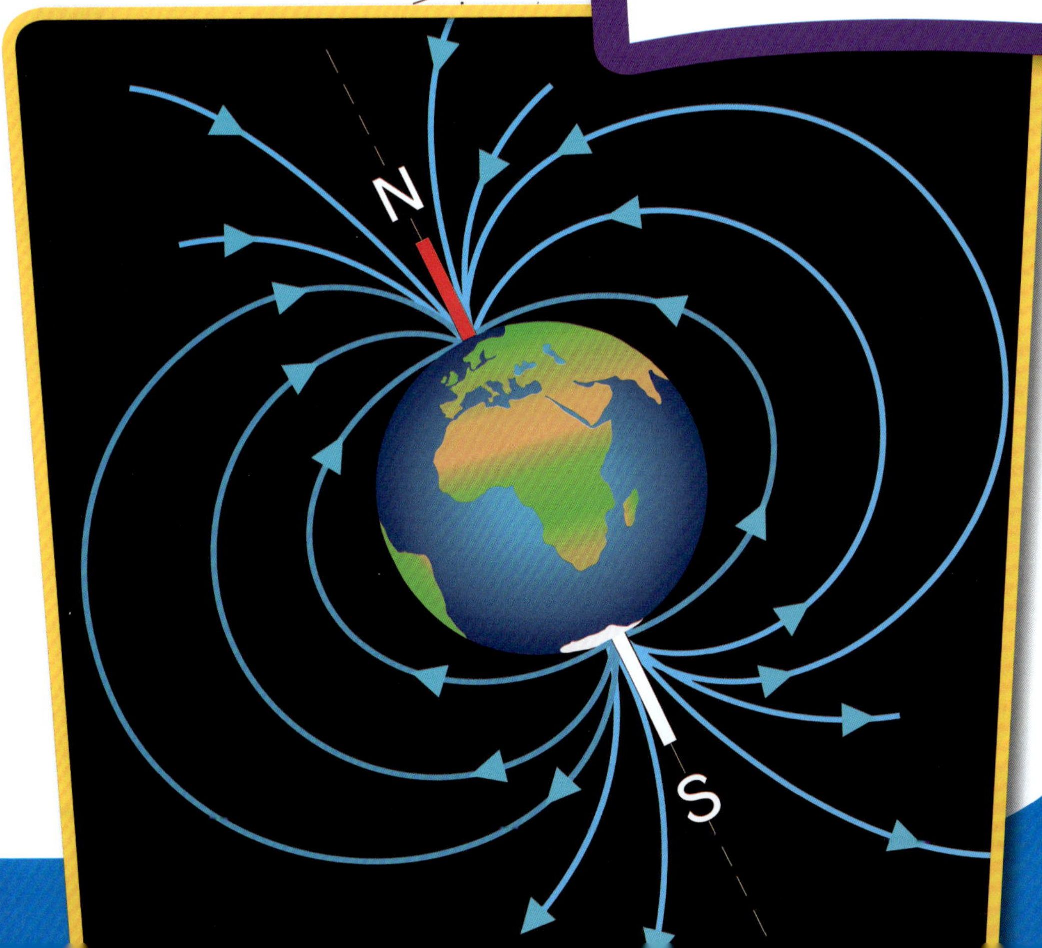

# Working for You

We need energy in our lives. Recycling items uses less energy than making brand-new items.

Less energy is needed to recycle a soda can than to make a can from new material.

You can help save energy, too. Turn off extra lights. Is the house a bit chilly? Do not turn up the heat. Put on a sweater instead. And do not forget to eat the right foods. Then, you will have plenty of energy to burn!

Adjusting the thermostat to a lower setting saves energy.

# Let's Do Science!

How does energy transfer? See for yourself!

## What to Get

- 1 larger marble
- 4 smaller marbles of the same size
- ruler with a groove

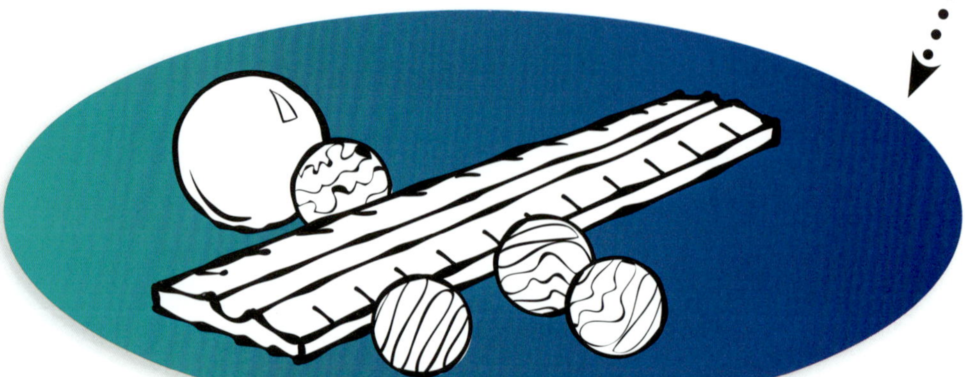

# What to Do

1. Place the ruler on a flat surface. Place two marbles of the same size on the ruler. Put them next to each other in the middle.

2. Place another same size marble at the end of the ruler. Roll it toward the other marbles. What happens? Try rolling it harder and softer.

3. Next, put one same size marble at either end of the ruler. Roll both at once toward the other marbles. What happens?

4. Put the large marble on one end of the ruler. What happens when you roll it toward the marbles in the middle?

# Glossary

**chemical energy**—energy that is stored in things like food and gas

**energy**—power that can be used to do something

**friction**—a force that slows motion

**light energy**—energy in the form of light, such as the sun

**magnetism**—the pull between certain metals

**sound energy**—energy that you can hear as it moves through the air

**static electricity**—electricity that collects on the surface of things and can cause a shock

**work**—something that is done when a force acts on an object

# Index


chemical energy, 11

electricity, 12–14, 22–24

friction, 20–21

heat energy, 18

light energy, 8

magnetism, 24

sound energy, 7

static electricity, 22–23

sun, 8, 10

water power, 14

wind power, 12

# Your Turn!

## Be an Energy Detective

What kinds of food give you the most energy? For 10 days, write what you eat for breakfast. Try to eat one thing for breakfast two or three days in a row. Then, change to a new food. Check your energy level three hours later. What is the best breakfast choice for you?